Recipes from a
Country Kitchen

Recipes from a
Country Kitchen

LIZ TRIGG

Photographs by Michelle Garrett

ULTIMATE
E D I T I O N S

First published in 1996 by Ultimate Editions

© Anness Publishing Limited 1996

Ultimate Editions is an imprint of
Anness Publishing Limited
1 Boundary Row
London SE1 8HP

This edition distributed in Canada by
Book Express, an imprint of
Raincoast Books Distribution Limited

ISBN 1-86035-089-5

Publisher: Joanna Lorenz
Project editor: Sarah Ainley
Designer: Janet James
Photographer: Michelle Garrett
Illustrator: Nadine Wickenden
Recipes pp. 8, 9, 16, 17, 30, 31, 48, 49 by
Katherine Richmond

Printed in Singapore by Star Standard Industries Pte. Ltd.

Contents

Spring Recipes

Spring brings the first of the year's tender young vegetables, and there are plenty of tempting recipes to make the most of seasonal produce. Treat yourself to a zesty lemon cake or an Easter plait studded with fruit and spices, for an Easter tea.

Pear and Watercress Soup with Stilton Croûtons

Pears and Stilton taste very good when you eat them together after the main course – here, for a change, they are served as a starter.

INGREDIENTS

1 bunch watercress
4 medium pears, sliced
900 ml / 1½ pints / 3¾ cups
chicken stock, preferably
home-made
salt and pepper
120 ml / 4 fl oz / ½ cup
double cream
juice of 1 lime

Croûtons
25 g / 1 oz / 2 tbsp butter
15 ml / 1 tbsp olive oil
200 g / 7 oz / 3 cups cubed
stale bread
140 g / 5 oz / 1 cup chopped
Stilton cheese

Serves 6

1

Keep back about a third of the watercress leaves. Place all the rest of the watercress leaves and stalks in a pan with the pears, stock and a little seasoning. Simmer for about 15–20 minutes. Reserving some watercress leaves for garnishing, add the rest of the leaves and immediately blend in a food processor until smooth.

2

Put the mixture into a bowl and stir in the cream and the lime juice to mix the flavours thoroughly. Season again to taste. Pour all the soup back into a pan and reheat, stirring gently until warmed through.

3

To make the croûtons, melt the butter and oil and fry the bread cubes until golden brown. Drain on kitchen paper. Put the cheese on top and heat under a hot grill until bubbling. Reheat the soup and pour into bowls. Divide the croûtons and remaining watercress between the bowls.

Spinach, Cognac, Garlic and Chicken Pâté

Pâté is an easy starter, as it can be made well in advance. This smooth version is delicious with warm brown rolls and butter or garlic bread.

INGREDIENTS

12 slices streaky bacon
25 g / 1 oz / 2 tbsp butter
1 onion, peeled and chopped
1 clove garlic, peeled and crushed
285 g / 10 oz frozen spinach,
thawed
50 g / 2 oz / ¾ cup wholemeal
breadcrumbs
30 ml / 2 tbsp Cognac
500 g / 1 lb minced chicken
(dark and light meat)
500 g / 1 lb minced pork
2 eggs, beaten
30 ml / 2 tbsp chopped mixed fresh
herbs,
such as parsley, sage and dill
salt and pepper

Serves 12

1

Fry the bacon in a pan until it is only just done, then arrange it round the sides of a 900 ml / 1½ pint / 1 US quart dish, if possible leaving a couple of slices to garnish.

3

Preheat the oven to 180°C / 350°F / Gas 4. Combine all the remaining ingredients, apart from any remaining bacon strips, in a bowl and mix well to blend. Spoon the pâté into the loaf tin and cover with any remaining bacon.

2

Melt the butter in a pan. Fry the onion and garlic until soft. Squeeze the spinach to remove as much water as possible, then add to the pan, stirring until the spinach is dry.

4

Cover the tin with a double thickness of foil and set it in a baking pan. Pour 2.5 cm / 1 in boiling water into the baking pan. Bake for about 1¼ hours. Remove the pâté and let it cool. Place a heavy weight on top of the pâté and refrigerate overnight.

Spring Roasted Chicken with Fresh Herbs and Garlic

A smaller chicken or four poussins can also be roasted in this way.

INGREDIENTS

*1.75 kg / 4½ lb free-range chicken
or 4 small poussins
finely grated rind and
juice of 1 lemon
1 garlic clove, crushed
30 ml / 2 tbsp olive oil
2 fresh thyme sprigs
2 fresh sage sprigs
75 g / 3 oz / 6 tbsp unsalted butter,
softened
salt and freshly ground
black pepper*

Serves 4

1

Season the chicken or poussins well.
Mix the lemon rind and juice, garlic and
olive oil together and pour them over the
chicken. Leave to marinate for at least
2 hours in a non-metallic dish.
When the chicken has marinated preheat
the oven to 230°C / 450°F / Gas Mark 8.

2

Place the herbs in the cavity of the bird and
smear the butter over the skin. Season well.
Roast the chicken for 10 minutes, then turn
the oven down to 190°C / 375°F / Gas Mark 5.
Baste the chicken well, and then roast for a
further 1 hour 30 minutes, until the juices run
clear when the thigh is pierced with a skewer.
Leave to rest for 15 minutes before carving.

Lemon and Rosemary Lamb Chops

*Spring lamb is delicious with the fresh flavour of lemon. Garnish with sprigs of
fresh rosemary — the aroma is irresistible.*

INGREDIENTS

*12 lamb cutlets
45 ml / 3 tbsp olive oil
2 large rosemary sprigs
juice of 1 lemon
3 garlic cloves, sliced
salt and freshly ground
black pepper*

Serves 4

1

Trim the excess fat from the cutlets.
Mix the oil, rosemary, lemon juice and
garlic together and season well.

2

Pour over the chops in a shallow dish and
marinate for 30 minutes. Remove from the
marinade, and blot the excess with kitchen
paper and grill for 10 minutes on each side.

Carrot and Coriander Soufflés

Use tender young carrots for this light-as-air dish.

INGREDIENTS

450 g / 1 lb carrots
30 ml / 2 tbsp fresh chopped coriander
4 eggs, separated
salt and freshly ground black pepper

Serves 4

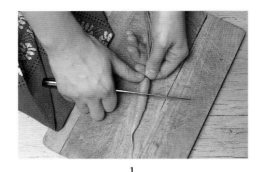

1

Peel the carrots.

2

Cook in boiling salted water for 20 minutes or until tender. Drain, and process until smooth in a food processor.

3

Preheat the oven to 200°C / 400°F / Gas Mark 6. Season the puréed carrots well, and stir in the chopped coriander.

4

Fold the egg yolks into the carrot mixture.

5

In a separate bowl, whisk the egg whites until stiff.

6

Fold the egg whites into the carrot mixture and pour into four greased ramekins. Bake for about 20 minutes or until risen and golden. Serve immediately.

Leeks with Ham and Cheese Sauce

A tasty teatime or supper dish: use a strong cheese for best results.

INGREDIENTS

4 leeks
4 slices ham

For the sauce
25 g / 1 oz / 2 tbsp unsalted butter
25 g / 1 oz / 1 tbsp plain flour
300 ml / ½ pint / 1¼ cups milk
½ tsp French mustard
115 g / 4 oz hard cheese, grated
salt and freshly ground
black pepper

Serves 4

1

Preheat the oven to 190°C / 375°F / Gas Mark 5. Trim the leeks to 2 cm / 1 in of the white and cook in salted water for about 20 minutes until soft. Drain thoroughly. Wrap the leeks in the ham slices.

2

To make the sauce, melt the butter in a saucepan. Add the flour and cook for a few minutes. Remove from the heat and gradually add the milk, whisking well with each addition. Return to the heat and whisk until the sauce thickens. Stir in the mustard and 75 g / 3 oz of the cheese and season well. Lay the leeks in a shallow ovenproof dish and pour over the sauce. Scatter the extra cheese on top and bake for 20 minutes.

Baked Eggs with Double Cream and Chives

This is a rich dish best served with Melba toast: it's very easy and quick to make.

INGREDIENTS

15 g / ½ oz / 1 tbsp unsalted
butter, softened
60 ml / 4 tbsp double cream
15 ml / 1 tbsp snipped fresh chives
4 eggs
50 g / 2 oz Gruyère cheese,
finely grated
salt and freshly ground
black pepper

Serves 2

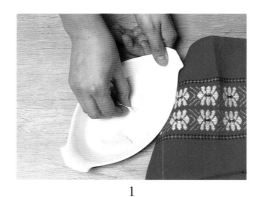

1

Preheat the oven to 180°C / 350°F / Gas Mark 4. Grease two individual gratin dishes. Mix the cream with the chives, and season with salt and pepper.

2

Break the eggs into each dish and top with the cream mixture. Sprinkle the cheese around the edges of the dishes and bake in the oven for 15–20 minutes. When cooked, brown the tops under the grill for a minute.

Courgette and Carrot Ribbons with Brie, Black Pepper and Parsley

This recipe produces a delicious vegetarian meal, or simply a new way of presenting colourful vegetables as an accompaniment to a main course.

INGREDIENTS

1 large green pepper, diced
15 ml / 1 tbsp sunflower oil
225 g / 8 oz Brie cheese
30 ml / 2 tbsp crème fraîche
5 ml / 1 tsp lemon juice
60 ml / 4 tbsp milk
10 ml / 2 tsp freshly ground black pepper
30 ml / 2 tbsp parsley, very finely chopped, plus extra to garnish
salt and pepper
6 large courgettes
6 large carrots

Serves 4

1

Sauté the green pepper in the sunflower oil until just tender. Place the remaining ingredients, apart from the carrots and courgettes, in a food processor and blend well. Place the mixture in a saucepan and add the green pepper.

2

Peel the courgettes. Use a potato peeler to slice them into long, thin strips. Do the same thing with the carrots. Put the courgettes and carrots in separate saucepans, cover with just enough water to cover, then simmer for 3 minutes until barely cooked.

3

Heat the sauce and pour into a shallow vegetable dish. Toss the courgette and carrot strips together and arrange them in the sauce. Garnish with a little finely chopped parsley.

Stuffed Tomatoes, with Wild Rice, Corn and Coriander

These tomatoes could be served as a light meal with crusty bread and a salad, or as an accompaniment to most meats or fish.

INGREDIENTS

8 medium tomatoes
50 g / 2 oz / ⅓ cup sweetcorn kernels
30 ml / 2 tbsp white wine
50 g / 2 oz / ¼ cup cooked wild rice
1 clove garlic
50 g / 2 oz / ½ cup grated Cheddar cheese
15 ml / 1 tbsp chopped fresh coriander
salt and pepper
15 ml / 1 tbsp olive oil

Serves 4

1

Cut the tops off the tomatoes and remove the seeds with a small teaspoon. Scoop out all the flesh and chop finely – also chop the tops.

2

Preheat the oven to 180°C / 350°F / Gas 4. Put the chopped tomato in a pan. Add the sweetcorn and the white wine. Cover with a close-fitting lid and simmer until tender. Drain.

3

Mix together all the remaining ingredients except the olive oil, adding salt and pepper to taste. Carefully spoon the mixture into the tomatoes, piling it higher in the centre. Sprinkle the oil over the top, arrange the tomatoes in an ovenproof dish, and bake at 180°C / 350°F / Gas 4 for 15–20 minutes until cooked through.

Lemon Drizzle Cake

You can also make this recipe using a large orange instead of the lemons;
either way, it makes a zesty treat for afternoon tea.

INGREDIENTS

finely grated rind of 2 lemons
175 g / 6 oz / 12 tbsp caster sugar
225 g / 8 oz / 1 cup unsalted
butter, softened
4 eggs
225 g / 8 oz / 2 cups self-raising
flour
5 ml / 1 tsp baking powder
1/4 tsp salt
shredded rind of 1 lemon,
to decorate

For the syrup
juice of 1 lemon
150 g / 5 oz / 3/4 cup caster sugar

Serves 6

1

Preheat the oven to 160°C / 325°F /
Gas Mark 3. Grease a 1 kg / 2 lb loaf tin or
18–20 cm / 7–8 in round cake tin and line it
with greaseproof paper or baking parchment.
Mix the lemon rind and caster sugar together.

2

Cream the butter with the lemon and sugar
mixture. Add the eggs and mix until
smooth. Sift the flour, baking powder and
salt into a bowl and fold a third at a time into
the mixture. Turn the batter into the tin,
smooth the top and bake for 1½ hours or
until golden brown and springy to the touch.

3

To make the syrup, slowly heat the juice
with the sugar and dissolve it gently. Make
several slashes in the top of the cake and pour
over the syrup. Sprinkle the shredded lemon
rind and 5 ml / 1 tsp granulated sugar on top
and leave to cool.

Wholemeal Bread

Home-made bread creates one of the most evocative smells in country cooking.
Eat this on the day of making, to enjoy the superb fresh taste.

INGREDIENTS

20 g / ¾ oz fresh yeast
300 ml / ½ pint / 1¼ cups
lukewarm milk
5 ml / 1 tsp caster sugar
225 g / 8 oz / 1½ cups strong
wholemeal flour, sifted
225 g / 8 oz / 2 cups strong
white flour, sifted
5 ml / 1 tsp salt
50 g / 2 oz / 4 tbsp butter,
chilled and cubed
1 egg, lightly beaten
30 ml / 2 tbsp mixed seeds

Makes 4 rounds or 2 loaves

1

Gently dissolve the yeast with a little of the milk and the sugar to make a paste. Place both the flours plus any bran from the sieve and the salt in a large warmed mixing bowl. Rub in the butter until the mixture resembles breadcrumbs.

2

Add the yeast mixture, remaining milk and egg and mix into a fairly soft dough. Knead on a floured board for 15 minutes. Lightly grease the mixing bowl and put the dough back in the bowl, covering it with a piece of greased cling film. Leave to double in size in a warm place (this should take at least an hour).

3

Knock the dough back and knead it for a further 10 minutes. Preheat the oven to 200°C / 400°F / Gas Mark 6. To make round loaves, divide the dough into four pieces and shape them into flattish rounds. Place them on a floured baking sheet and leave to rise for a further 15 minutes. Sprinkle the loaves with the mixed seeds. Bake for about 20 minutes until golden and firm.

NOTE

For tin-shaped loaves, put the knocked-back dough into two greased loaf tins instead. Leave to rise for a further 45 minutes and then bake for about 45 minutes, until the loaf sounds hollow when turned out of the tin and knocked on the base.

Easter Plait

Serve this delicious plait sliced with butter and jam.
It is also very good toasted on the day after you made it.

INGREDIENTS

200 ml / 7 fl oz / ⅞ cup milk
2 eggs, lightly beaten
450 g / 1 lb / 4 cups plain flour
½ tsp salt
10 ml / 2 tsp ground mixed spice
75 g / 3 oz / 6 tbsp butter
20 g / ¾ oz dried yeast
75 g / 3 oz / 6 tbsp caster sugar

175 g / 6 oz / 1¼ cups currants
25 g / 1 oz / ¼ cup candied mixed
peel, chopped
a little sweetened milk, to glaze
25 g / 1 oz / 1½ tbsp glacé
cherries, chopped
15 g / ½ oz / 1 tbsp angelica,
chopped

Serves 8

1

Warm the milk to lukewarm, add two-thirds
of it to the eggs and mix well.

2

Sift the flour, salt and mixed spice together.
Rub in the butter, then add the sugar
and dried yeast. Make a well in the centre,
and add the milk mixture, adding more milk
as necessary to make a sticky dough.

3

Knead on a well-floured surface and then
knead in the currants and mixed peel,
reserving 15 ml / 1 tbsp for the topping. Put
the dough in a lightly greased bowl and
cover it with a damp tea towel. Leave to
double its size. Preheat the oven to
220°C / 425°F / Gas Mark 7.

4

Turn the dough out on to a floured surface
and knead again for 2–3 minutes. Divide the
dough into three even pieces. Roll each
piece into a sausage shape roughly
20 cm / 8 in long. Plait the three pieces
together, turning under and pinching each
end. Place on a floured baking sheet and
leave to rise for 15 minutes.

5

Brush the top with sweetened milk and
scatter with roughly chopped cherries, strips
of angelica and the reserved mixed peel.
Bake in the preheated oven for 45 minutes or
until the bread sounds hollow when tapped
on the bottom. Cool slightly on a wire rack.

Orange-blossom Jelly

A fresh orange jelly makes a delightful dessert: the natural fruit flavour combined with the smooth jelly has a cleansing quality that is especially welcome after a rich main course. This is delicious served with thin, crisp langues de chat *biscuits.*

65 g / 2½ oz / 5 tbsp caster sugar
150 ml / ¼ pint / ⅔ cup water
2 sachets of gelatine
(about 25 g / 1 oz)
600 ml / 1 pint / 2½ cups freshly
squeezed orange juice
30 ml / 2 tbsp orange-flower water

Serves 4–6

1

Place the caster sugar and water in a small saucepan and gently heat to dissolve the sugar. Leave to cool.

2

Sprinkle over the gelatine, ensuring it is completely submerged in the water. Leave to stand until the gelatine has absorbed all the liquid and is solid.

3

Gently melt the gelatine over a bowl of simmering water until it becomes clear and transparent. Leave to cool. When the gelatine is cold, mix it with the orange juice and orange-flower water.

4

Wet a jelly mould and pour in the jelly. Chill in the refrigerator for at least 2 hours, or until set. Turn out to serve.

Rhubarb and Orange Crumble

The almonds give this crumble topping a nutty taste and crunchy texture.
This crumble is extra-delicious with home-made custard.

INGREDIENTS

900 g / 2 lb rhubarb, cut in
5 cm / 2 in lengths
75 g / 3 oz / 6 tbsp caster sugar
finely grated rind and juice
of 2 oranges

115 g / 4 oz / 1 cup plain flour
115 g / 4 oz / ½ cup unsalted
butter, chilled and cubed
75 g / 3 oz / 6 tbsp demerara sugar
115 g / 4 oz / 1¼ cups ground almonds

Serves 6

1

Preheat the oven to 180°C / 350°F /
Gas Mark 4. Place the rhubarb in a shallow
ovenproof dish.

2

Sprinkle over the caster sugar and add the
orange rind and juice.

3

Sift the flour into a mixing bowl and add the
butter. Rub the butter into the flour until
the mixture resembles breadcrumbs.

4

Add the demerara sugar and ground almonds
and mix well.

5

Spoon the crumble mixture over the fruit to
cover it completely. Bake for 40 minutes,
until the top is browned and the fruit is
cooked. Serve warm.

Summer Recipes

....

*The warm, lazy days and long nights of summer
provide the perfect excuse for outdoor dining
with friends and family. Try Mediterranean quiche
or a glorious garden salad with nasturtium flowers.
Cooling treats include strawberry fool, or
home-made mint ice cream.*

Mackerel with Roasted Blueberries

Fresh blueberries burst with flavour when roasted, and their sharpness complements the rich flesh of mackerel very well.

15 g / ½ oz / 2 tsp plain flour
4 small cooked, smoked mackerel fillets
50 g / 2 oz / 4 tbsp unsalted butter
juice of ½ lemon
salt and freshly ground black pepper

For the roasted blueberries
450 g / 1 lb blueberries
25 g / 1 oz / 2 tbsp caster sugar
15 g / ½ oz / 1 tbsp unsalted butter
salt and freshly ground black pepper

Serves 4

1

Preheat the oven to 200°C / 400°F / Gas Mark 6. Season the flour. Dip each fish fillet into the flour to coat it well.

2

Dot the butter on the fillets and bake in the oven for 20 minutes.

3

Place the blueberries, sugar, butter and seasoning in a separate small roasting tin and roast them, basting them occasionally, for 15 minutes. To serve, drizzle the lemon juice over the roasted mackerel, accompanied by the roasted blueberries.

Griddled Trout with Bacon

This dish can also be cooked on the barbecue.

INGREDIENTS

25 g / 1 oz / 1 tbsp plain flour
4 trout, cleaned and gutted
75 g / 3 oz streaky bacon
50 g / 2 oz / 4 tbsp butter
15 ml / 1 tbsp olive oil
juice of ½ lemon
salt and freshly ground
black pepper

Serves 4

1

Pat the trout dry with kitchen roll and
mix the flour and seasoning together.

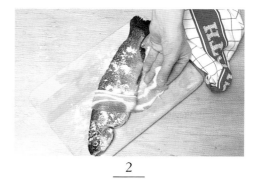

2

Roll the trout in the seasoned flour mixture
and wrap tightly in the streaky bacon.
Heat a heavy frying pan. Heat the butter and
oil in the pan and fry the trout for 5 minutes
on each side. Serve immediately, with the
lemon juice drizzled on top.

Lamb Steaks Marinated in Mint and Sherry

The marinade is the key to the success of this recipe. The sherry imparts a wonderful tang.

INGREDIENTS

6 large lamb steaks or 12 smaller chops

Marinade
30 ml / 2 tbsp chopped fresh mint leaves
15 ml / 1 tbsp black peppercorns
1 medium onion, chopped
120 ml / 4 fl oz / ½ cup sherry
60 ml / 2 fl oz / ¼ cup extra virgin olive oil
2 cloves garlic

Serves 6

1

Place the mint leaves and peppercorns in a food processor and blend until very finely chopped. Add the chopped onion and process again until smooth. Add the rest of the marinade ingredients and process until completely mixed. The marinade should be of a fairly thick consistency.

2

Place the steaks or chops in a shallow dish and pour on the marinade. Cover with non-PVC clear film and refrigerate overnight.

3

Grill or barbecue the steaks on a very high heat until cooked, basting occasionally with the marinade.

Broccoli and Cauliflower with Cider and Apple Mint Sauce

The cider sauce made here is also ideal for other vegetables, such as celery or beans. It is flavoured using tamari, a Japanese soy sauce, and apple mint.

INGREDIENTS

1 large onion, chopped
2 large carrots, chopped
1 large clove garlic
15 ml / 1 tbsp dill seed
4 large sprigs apple mint
30 ml / 2 tbsp olive oil
25 g / 1 oz / 2 tbsp plain flour
300 ml / ½ pint / 1¼ cups
dry cider
500 g / 1 lb broccoli florets
500 g / 1 lb cauliflower florets
30 ml / 2 tbsp tamari
10 ml / 2 tsp mint jelly

Serves 4

1

Sauté the onions, carrots, garlic, dill seeds and apple mint leaves in the olive oil until nearly cooked. Stir in the flour and cook for half a minute or so. Pour in the cider and simmer until the sauce looks glossy.

2

Boil the broccoli and cauliflower in separate pans until tender.

3

Pour the sauce into a food processor and add the tamari and the mint jelly. Blend until finely puréed. Pour over the broccoli and cauliflower.

Mediterranean Quiche

The strong Mediterranean flavours of tomatoes, peppers and anchovies complement beautifully the cheesy pastry in this unusual quiche.

INGREDIENTS

For the pastry
225 g / 8 oz / 2 cups plain flour
pinch of salt
pinch of dry mustard
115 g / 4 oz / ½ cup butter,
chilled and cubed
50 g / 2 oz Gruyère cheese, grated

For the filling
50 g / 2 oz can of anchovies in oil,
drained
50 ml / 2 fl oz / ¼ cup milk
30 ml / 2 tbsp French mustard
45 ml / 3 tbsp olive oil
2 large Spanish onions, sliced
1 red pepper, seeded and
very finely sliced
3 egg yolks
350 ml / 12 fl oz / 1½ cups
double cream
1 garlic clove, crushed
175 g / 6 oz mature Cheddar
cheese, grated
2 large tomatoes, thickly sliced
salt and freshly ground
black pepper
30 ml / 2 tbsp chopped fresh basil,
to garnish

Serves 12

1

First make the pastry. Place the flour, salt and mustard powder in a food processor, add the butter and process the mixture until it resembles breadcrumbs.

2

Add the cheese and process again briefly. Add enough iced water to make a stiff dough: it will be ready when the dough forms a ball. Wrap with cling film and chill for 30 minutes.

3

Meanwhile, make the filling. Soak the anchovies in the milk for 20 minutes. Drain away the milk.

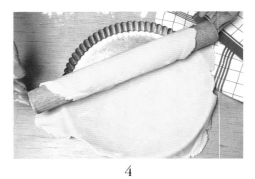

4

Roll out the chilled pastry and line a 23 cm / 9 in loose-based flan tin. Spread over the mustard and chill for a further 15 minutes.

5

Preheat the oven to 200°C / 400°F / Gas Mark 6. Heat the oil in a frying pan and cook the onions and red pepper until soft. In a separate bowl, beat the egg yolks, cream, garlic and Cheddar cheese together; season well. Arrange the tomatoes in a single layer in the pastry case. Top with the onion and pepper mixture and the anchovy fillets. Pour over the egg mixture. Bake for 30–35 minutes. Sprinkle over the basil and serve.

New Potato Salad

*Potatoes freshly dug up from the garden are the best. Always leave the skins on:
just wash the dirt away thoroughly. If you add the mayonnaise and other
ingredients when the potatoes are hot, the flavours will develop as the potatoes cool.*

INGREDIENTS

*900 g / 2 lb baby new potatoes
2 green apples, cored and chopped
4 spring onions, chopped
3 celery sticks, finely chopped
150 ml / ¼ pint / ⅔ cup
mayonnaise
salt and freshly ground
black pepper*

Serves 6

1

Cook the potatoes in salted, boiling water
for about 20 minutes, or until they are
very tender.

2

Drain the potatoes well and immediately add
the remaining ingredients and stir until well
mixed. Leave to cool and serve cold.

French Bean Salad

The secret of this recipe is to dress the beans while still hot.

INGREDIENTS

*175 g / 6 oz cherry tomatoes,
halved
5 ml / 1 tsp sugar
450 g / 1 lb French beans,
topped and tailed
175 g / 6 oz feta cheese, cubed
salt and freshly ground
black pepper*

For the dressing
*90 ml / 6 tbsp olive oil
45 ml / 3 tbsp white-wine vinegar
¼ tsp Dijon mustard
2 garlic cloves, crushed
salt and freshly ground
black pepper*

Serves 6

1

Preheat the oven to 230°C / 450°F /
Gas Mark 8. Put the cherry tomatoes on a
baking sheet and sprinkle over the sugar,
salt and pepper. Roast for 20 minutes,
then leave to cool. Meanwhile, cook the
beans in boiling, salted water for 10 minutes.

2

Make the dressing by whisking together the
oil, vinegar, mustard, garlic and seasoning.
Drain the beans and immediately pour over
the vinaigrette and mix well. When cool,
stir in the roasted tomatoes and the
feta cheese. Serve chilled.

Squash à la Greque

A traditional French-style dish that is usually made with mushrooms.
Make sure that you cook the baby squash until they are quite tender,
so they can fully absorb the delicious flavours of the marinade.

INGREDIENTS

175 g / 6 oz patty-pan squash
250 ml / 8 fl oz / 1 cup white wine
juice of 2 lemons
fresh thyme sprig
bay leaf
small bunch of fresh chervil,
roughly chopped
¼ tsp coriander seeds, crushed
¼ tsp black peppercorns, crushed
75 ml / 5 tbsp olive oil

Serves 4

1

Blanch the patty-pan squash in boiling
water for 3 minutes, and then refresh them
in cold water.

2

Place all the remaining ingredients in a pan,
add 150 ml / ½ pint / ⅔ cup of water and
simmer for 10 minutes, covered. Add the
patty-pans and cook for 10 minutes. Remove
with a slotted spoon when they are cooked
and tender to the bite.

3

Reduce the liquid by boiling hard for
10 minutes. Strain it and pour it over the
squashes. Leave until cool for the flavours to
be absorbed. Serve cold.

Garden Salad

You can use any fresh, edible flowers from your garden for this beautiful salad.

INGREDIENTS

1 cos lettuce
175 g / 6 oz rocket
1 small frisée lettuce
fresh chervil and tarragon sprigs
15 ml / 1 tbsp snipped fresh chives
handful of mixed edible flower
heads, such as nasturtiums
or marigolds

For the dressing
45 ml / 3 tbsp olive oil
15 ml / 1 tbsp white-wine vinegar
½ tsp French mustard
1 garlic clove, crushed
pinch of sugar

Serves 4

1

Mix the cos, rocket and frisée leaves
and herbs together.

2

Make the dressing by whisking all the
ingredients together in a large bowl. Toss the
salad leaves in the bowl with the dressing,
add the flower heads and serve at once.

Country Strawberry Fool

Make this delicious fool on the day you want to eat it, and chill it well,
for the best strawberry taste.

INGREDIENTS

300 ml / ½ pint / 1¼ cups milk
2 egg yolks
90 g / 3½ oz / scant ½ cup
caster sugar
few drops of vanilla essence
900 g / 2 lb ripe strawberries
juice of ½ lemon
300 ml / ½ pint / 1¼ cups double
cream

To decorate
12 small strawberries
4 fresh mint sprigs

Serves 4

1

First make the custard. Whisk 30 ml / 2 tbsp milk with the egg yolks, 15 ml / 1 tbsp caster sugar and the vanilla essence.

2

Heat the remaining milk until it is just below boiling point.

3

Stir the milk into the egg mixture. Rinse the pan out and return the mixture to it.

4

Gently heat and whisk until the mixture thickens (it should be thick enough to coat the back of a spoon). Lay a wet piece of greaseproof paper on top of the custard and leave it to cool.

5

Purée the strawberries in a food processor or blender with the lemon juice and the remaining sugar.

6

Lightly whip the cream and fold in the fruit purée and custard. Pour into glass dishes and decorate with the whole strawberries and sprigs of mint.

Mint Ice Cream

This ice cream is best served slightly softened, so take it out
of the freezer 20 minutes before you want to serve it. For a special occasion,
this looks spectacular served in an ice bowl.

INGREDIENTS

8 egg yolks
75 g / 3 oz / 6 tbsp caster sugar
600 ml / 1 pint / 2½ cups single
cream
1 vanilla pod
60 ml / 4 tbsp chopped fresh mint

Serves 8

1

Beat the egg yolks and sugar until they are
pale and light using a hand-held electric
beater or a balloon whisk. Transfer to a
small saucepan.

2

In a separate saucepan, bring the cream to
the boil with the vanilla pod.

3

Remove the vanilla pod and pour the hot cream
on to the egg mixture, whisking briskly.

4

Continue whisking to ensure the eggs
are mixed into the cream.

5

Gently heat the mixture until the custard
thickens enough to coat the back of a
wooden spoon. Leave to cool.

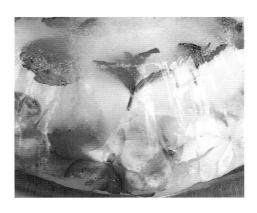

6

Stir in the mint and place in an ice-cream
maker to churn, about 3–4 hours. If you
don't have an ice-cream maker, freeze the
ice cream until mushy and then whisk it well
again, to break down the ice crystals. Freeze
for another 3 hours until it is softly frozen
and whisk again. Finally freeze until hard:
at least 6 hours.

Mixed Berry Tart

The orange-flavoured pastry is delicious with the fresh fruits of summer.
Serve this with some extra shreds of orange rind scattered on top.

INGREDIENTS

For the pastry
225 g / 8 oz / 2 cups plain flour
115 g / 4 oz / ½ cup unsalted
butter
finely grated rind of 1 orange,
plus extra to decorate

For the filling
300 ml / ½ pint / 1 ¼ cups
crème fraîche
finely grated rind of 1 lemon
10 ml / 2 tsp icing sugar
675 g / 1 ½ lb mixed
summer berries

Serves 8

1

To make the pastry, put the flour and butter
in a large bowl. Rub in the butter until the
mixture resembles breadcrumbs.

2

Add the orange rind and enough cold water
to make a soft dough.

3

Roll into a ball and chill for at least
30 minutes. Roll out the pastry on a
lightly floured surface.

4

Line a 23 cm / 9 in loose-based flan tin with
the pastry. Chill for 30 minutes. Preheat the
oven to 200°C / 400°F / Gas Mark 6 and
place a baking sheet in the oven to heat up.
Line the tin with greaseproof paper and
baking beans and bake blind on the baking
sheet for 15 minutes. Remove the paper
and beans and bake for 10 minutes more,
until the pastry is golden. Allow to
cool completely. To make the filling,
whisk the crème fraîche, lemon rind and
sugar together and pour into the pastry case.
Top with fruit, sprinkle with orange
rind and serve sliced.

Autumn Recipes

....

*Reap the benefits of the autumn harvest with this
collection of recipes; wild mushroom tart,
thyme-roasted onions and duck and chestnut casserole
all make the most of autumn produce.
Warming desserts such as steamed ginger and
syrup pudding or poached pears, are guaranteed to
keep away the autumn chill.*

Wild Mushroom Tart

The flavour of wild mushrooms makes this tart really rich: use as wide a variety of mushrooms as you can get.

INGREDIENTS

For the pastry
225 g / 8 oz / 2 cups plain flour
50 g / 2 oz / 4 tbsp hard white fat
10 ml / 2 tsp lemon juice
about 150 ml / ¼ pint / ⅔ cup
ice-cold water
115 g / 4 oz / ½ cup butter,
chilled and cubed
1 egg, beaten, to glaze

For the filling
150 g / 5 oz / 10 tbsp butter
2 shallots, finely chopped
2 garlic cloves, crushed
450 g / 1 lb mixed wild
mushrooms, sliced
45 ml / 3 tbsp chopped fresh parsley
30 ml / 2 tbsp double cream
salt and freshly ground
black pepper

Serves 6

1

To make the pastry, sieve the flour and ½ tsp salt together into a large bowl. Add the white fat and rub into the mixture until it resembles breadcrumbs.

2

Add the lemon juice and enough iced water to make a soft but not sticky dough. Cover and chill for 20 minutes.

3

Roll the pastry out into a rectangle on a lightly floured surface. Mark the dough into three equal strips and arrange half the butter cubes over two-thirds of the dough.

4

Fold the outer two-thirds over, folding over the uncovered third last. Seal the edges with a rolling pin. Give the dough a quarter turn and roll it out again. Mark it into thirds and dot with the remaining butter cubes in the same way.

5

Chill the pastry for 20 minutes. Repeat the process of marking into thirds, folding over, giving a quarter turn and rolling out three times, chilling for 20 minutes in between each time. To make the filling, melt 50 g / 2 oz / 4 tbsp butter and fry the shallots and garlic until soft but not browned. Add the remaining butter and the mushrooms and cook for 35–40 minutes. Drain off any excess liquid and stir in the remaining ingredients. Leave to cool. Preheat the oven to 220°C / 450°F / Gas Mark 7.

6

Divide the pastry in two. Roll out one half into a 22 cm / 9 in round, cutting around a plate to make a neat shape. Pile the filling into the centre. Roll out the remaining pastry large enough to cover the base. Brush the edges of the base with water and then lay the second pastry circle on top. Press the edges together to seal and brush the top with a little beaten egg. Bake for 45 minutes, or until the pastry is risen, golden and flaky.

Turkey with Apples, Bay and Madeira

This casserole will win you many compliments without the worry of a complicated menu. The unusual apple garnish looks very attractive.

INGREDIENTS

*750 g / 1 1/2 lb turkey breast fillets, cut into 2 cm / 3/4 in slices
salt and pepper
50 g / 2 oz / 4 tbsp butter, plus another 15 g / 1/2 oz / 1 tbsp for the apple garnish
4 tart apples, peeled and sliced
60 ml / 2 fl oz / 4 tbsp Madeira, plus another 30 ml / 1 fl oz / 2 tbsp for the apple garnish
150 ml / 1/4 pint / 2/3 cup chicken stock
3 bay leaves
10 ml / 2 tsp cornflour
150 ml / 1/4 pint / 2/3 cup double cream*

Serves 4

1

Season the turkey, melt 25 g / 1 oz / 2 tbsp the butter in a pan and fry the meat to seal it. Transfer to a casserole. Preheat the oven to 180°C / 350°F / Gas 4. Add the remaining butter to the pan with two sliced apples, and cook gently for 1–2 minutes.

3

Blend the cornflour with a little of the cream, then add the rest of the cream. Add this mixture to the casserole and return to the oven for 10 minutes to allow the sauce to thicken.

2

Add the Madeira, stock and bay leaves to the turkey and stir in. Simmer for another couple of minutes. Cover the casserole and bake for about 40 minutes.

4

To make the garnish, melt 25 g / 1 oz / 2 tbsp butter in a pan and gently fry the apple slices. Add the Madeira and set it alight. Once the flames have died down continue to fry the apple until it is lightly browned, and garnish the casserole with it.

Chicken with Sloe Gin and Juniper

Juniper is used in the manufacture of gin, and the reinforcement of the flavour by using both sloe gin and juniper is delicious. Sloe gin is easy to make, but can also be bought ready-made.

INGREDIENTS

25 g / 1 oz / 2 tbsp butter
30 ml / 2 tbsp sunflower oil
8 chicken breast fillets
350 g / 12 oz carrots, cooked
1 clove garlic, peeled and crushed
15 ml / 1 tbsp finely chopped parsley
60 ml / 2 fl oz / ¼ cup chicken stock
60 ml / 2 fl oz / ¼ cup sloe gin
60 ml / 2 fl oz / ¼ cup red wine
5 ml / 1 tsp crushed juniper berries
salt and pepper
1 bunch basil, to garnish

Serves 8

1

Melt the butter with the oil in a pan, and sauté the chicken until browned on all sides.

2

In a food processor, combine all the remaining ingredients except the watercress, and blend to a smooth purée. If the mixture seems too thick add a little more red wine or water until a thinner consistency is reached.

3

Put the chicken breasts in a pan, pour the sauce over the top and cool until the chicken is cooked through – about 15 minutes. Adjust the seasoning and serve garnished with chopped fresh basil.

Mushroom and Parsley Soup

Thickened with bread, this rich mushroom soup will warm you up
on cold autumn days. It makes a terrific hearty lunch.

INGREDIENTS

75 g / 3 oz / 6 tbsp unsalted butter
900 g / 2 lb field mushrooms,
sliced
2 onions, roughly chopped
600 ml / 1 pint / 2½ cups milk
8 slices white bread
60 ml / 4 tbsp chopped fresh parsley
300 ml / ½ pint / 1¼ cups
double cream
salt and freshly ground
black pepper

Serves 8

1

Melt the butter and sauté the mushrooms
and onions until soft but not coloured –
about 10 minutes. Add the milk.

2

Tear the bread into pieces, drop them into
the soup and leave the bread to soak for
15 minutes. Purée the soup and return it to
the pan. Add the parsley, cream and seasoning.
Re-heat, but do not allow the soup to boil.
Serve at once.

Thyme-roasted Onions

These slowly roasted onions develop a delicious, sweet flavour which is perfect
with roast meat. You could prepare par-boiled new potatoes in the same way.

INGREDIENTS

75 ml / 5 tbsp olive oil
50 g / 2 oz / 4 tbsp unsalted butter
900 g / 2 lb small onions
30 ml / 2 tbsp chopped fresh thyme
salt and freshly ground
black pepper

Serves 4

1

Preheat the oven to 220°C / 425°F /
Gas Mark 7. Heat the oil and butter in a
large roasting tin. Add the onions and toss
them in the oil and butter mixture.

2

Add the thyme and seasoning and roast for
45 minutes, basting regularly.

Duck and Chestnut Casserole

Serve this casserole with a mixture of mashed potatoes and celeriac,
to soak up the rich duck juices.

INGREDIENTS

1.75 kg / 4½ lb duck
45 ml / 3 tbsp olive oil
175 g / 6 oz small onions
50 g / 2 oz field mushrooms
50 g / 2 oz shiitake mushrooms
300 ml / ½ pint / 1¼ cups
red wine
300 ml / ½ pint / 1¼ cups
beef stock
225 g / 8 oz canned, peeled,
unsweetened chestnuts, drained
salt and freshly ground
black pepper

Serves 4–6

1

Joint the duck into eight pieces. Heat the oil
in a large frying pan and brown the duck
pieces. Remove from the frying pan.

2

Add the onions to the pan and brown them
well for 10 minutes.

3

Add the mushrooms and cook for a few
minutes more. Deglaze the pan with the
red wine and boil to reduce the volume
by half. Meanwhile, preheat the oven to
180°C / 350°F / Gas Mark 4.

4

Pour the wine and the stock into a
casserole. Replace the duck, add the
chestnuts, season well and cook in the oven
for 1½ hours.

Cheese Scones

These delicious scones make a good tea-time treat. They are best served fresh and still slightly warm.

INGREDIENTS

225 g / 8 oz / 2 cups plain flour
12 ml / 2½ tsp baking powder
½ tsp dry mustard powder
½ tsp salt
50 g / 2 oz / 4 tbsp butter, chilled
75 g / 3 oz Cheddar cheese, grated
150 ml / ¼ pint / ⅔ cup milk
1 egg, beaten

Makes 12

1	2
Preheat the oven to 230°C / 450°F / Gas Mark 8. Sift the flour, baking powder, mustard powder and salt into a mixing bowl. Add the butter and rub it into the flour mixture until the mixture resembles breadcrumbs. Stir in 50 g / 2 oz of the cheese.	Make a well in the centre and add the milk and egg. Mix gently and then turn the dough out on to a lightly floured surface. Roll it out and cut it into triangles or squares. Brush lightly with milk and sprinkle with the remaining cheese. Leave to rest for 15 minutes, then bake them for 15 minutes, or until well risen.

Oatcakes

These are very simple to make and are an excellent addition to a cheese board.

INGREDIENTS

225 g / 8 oz / 1⅔ cups medium oatmeal
75 g / 3 oz / ¾ cup plain flour
¼ tsp bicarbonate of soda
5 ml / 1 tsp salt
25 g / 1 oz / 2 tbsp hard white vegetable fat
25 g / 1 oz / 2 tbsp butter

Makes 24

1	2
Preheat the oven to 220°C / 425°F / Gas Mark 7. Place the oatmeal, flour, soda and salt in a large bowl. Gently melt the two fats together in a pan.	Add the melted fat and enough boiling water to make a soft dough. Turn out on to a surface scattered with a little oatmeal. Roll out the dough thinly and cut it into circles. Bake the oatcakes on ungreased baking trays for 15 minutes, until crisp.

Blackberry Charlotte

A classic pudding, perfect for cold days. Serve with lightly whipped cream or home-made custard.

INGREDIENTS

65 g / 2½ oz / 5 tbsp unsalted butter
175 g / 6 oz / 3 cups fresh white breadcrumbs
50 g / 2 oz / 4 tbsp soft brown sugar
60 ml / 4 tbsp golden syrup
finely grated rind and juice of 2 lemons
50 g / 2 oz walnut halves
450 g / 1 lb blackberries
450 g / 1 lb cooking apples, peeled, cored and finely sliced

Serves 4

1

Preheat the oven to 180°C / 350°F / Gas Mark 4. Grease a 450 ml / ¾ pint / 2 cup dish with 15 g / ½ oz / 1 tbsp of the butter. Melt the remaining butter and add the breadcrumbs. Sauté them for 5–7 minutes, until the crumbs are a little crisp and golden. Leave to cool slightly.

2

Place the sugar, syrup, lemon rind and juice in a small saucepan and gently warm them. Add the crumbs.

3

Process the walnuts until they are finely ground.

4

Arrange a thin layer of blackberries on the dish. Top with a thin layer of crumbs.

5

Add a thin layer of apple, topping it with another thin layer of crumbs. Repeat the process with another layer of blackberries, followed by a layer of crumbs. Continue until you have used up all the ingredients, finishing with a layer of crumbs.

The mixture should be piled well above the top edge of the dish, because it shrinks during cooking. Bake for 30 minutes, until the crumbs are golden and the fruit is soft.

Poached Pears

Serve warm with clotted cream and crisp shortbread fingers.

INGREDIENTS

6 medium pears
350 g / 12 oz / 1¾ cups caster
sugar
75 ml / 5 tbsp runny honey
1 vanilla pod
600 ml / 1 pint / 2½ cups red wine
5 ml / 1 tsp whole cloves
7 cm / 3 in cinnamon stick

Serves 4

1

Peel the pears but leave them whole,
keeping the stalks as well.

2

Put the sugar, honey, vanilla pod, wine,
cloves and cinnamon stick in a large pan.

3

Add the pears and poach until soft, about
30 minutes. When the pears are tender,
remove them with a slotted spoon and keep
them warm. Remove the vanilla pod, cloves
and cinnamon stick and boil the liquid
until it is reduced by half. Serve spooned
over the pears.

Steamed Ginger and Cinnamon Syrup Pudding

A traditional and comforting steamed pudding, best served with custard.

INGREDIENTS

*120 g / 4½ oz / 9 tbsp softened
butter
45 ml / 3 tbsp golden syrup
115 g / 4 oz / ½ cup caster sugar
2 eggs, lightly beaten
115 g / 4 oz / 1 cup plain flour
5 ml / 1 tsp baking powder
5 ml / 1 tsp ground cinnamon
25 g / 1 oz stem ginger,
finely chopped
30 ml / 2 tbsp milk*

Serves 4

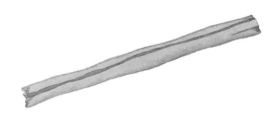

1

Set a full steamer or saucepan of water on to boil. Lightly grease a 600 ml / 1 pint / 2½ cup pudding basin with 15 g / ½ oz / 1 tbsp butter. Place the golden syrup in the basin.

2

Cream the remaining butter and sugar together until light and fluffy. Gradually add the eggs until the mixture is glossy. Sift the flour, baking powder and cinnamon together and fold them into the mixture, with the stem ginger. Add the milk to make a soft, dropping consistency.

3

Spoon the batter into the basin and smooth the top. Cover with a pleated piece of greaseproof paper, to allow for expansion during cooking. Tie securely with string and steam for 1½–2 hours, making sure that the water level is kept topped up, to ensure a good flow of steam to cook the pudding. Turn the pudding out to serve it.

French Apple Tart

For added flavour, scatter some toasted, flaked almonds over the top of this classic tart.

INGREDIENTS

For the pastry
115 g / 4 oz / ½ cup unsalted butter, softened
50 g / 2 oz / 4 tbsp vanilla sugar
1 egg
225 g / 8 oz / 2 cups plain flour

For the filling
50 g / 2 oz / 4 tbsp unsalted butter
5 large tart apples, peeled, cored and sliced
juice of ½ lemon
300 ml / ½ pint / 1¼ cups double cream
2 egg yolks
25 g / 1 oz / 2 tbsp vanilla sugar
50 g / 2 oz / ⅔ cup ground almonds, toasted
25 g / 1 oz / 2 tbsp flaked almonds, toasted, to garnish

Serves 8

1

Place the butter and sugar in a food processor and process them well together. Add the egg and process to mix it in well.

2

Add the flour and process till you have a soft dough. Wrap the dough in cling film and chill it for 30 minutes.

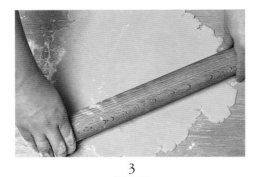

3

Roll the pastry out on a lightly floured surface to about 22–25 cm / 9–10 in diameter.

4

Line a flan tin with the pastry and chill it for a further 30 minutes. Preheat the oven to 220°C / 425°F / Gas Mark 7 and place a baking sheet in the oven to heat up. Line the pastry case with greaseproof paper and baking beans and bake blind on the baking sheet for 10 minutes. Then remove the beans and paper and cook for a further 5 minutes.

5

Turn the oven down to 190°C / 375°F / Gas Mark 5. To make the filling, melt the butter in a frying pan and lightly sauté the apples for 5–7 minutes. Sprinkle the apples with lemon juice.

6

Beat the cream and egg yolks with the sugar. Stir in the toasted ground almonds. Arrange the apple slices on top of the warm pastry and pour over the cream mixture. Bake for 25 minutes, or until the cream is just about set – it tastes better if the cream is still slightly runny in the centre. Serve hot or cold, scattered with flaked almonds.

Winter Recipes

With the nights drawing in, we all need something
substantial and warming to keep out the cold.
Try roast beef with roasted peppers, or raised
country pie. Scotch pancakes or cranberry muffins
are a perfect fire-side treat, and rich Christmas
pudding is the perfect way to round off the year.

Roast Beef with Porcini and Roasted Sweet Peppers

A substantial and warming dish for cold, dark evenings.

INGREDIENTS

1.5 kg / 3–3½ lb piece of sirloin
15 ml / 1 tbsp olive oil
450 g / 1 lb small red peppers
115 g / 4 oz mushrooms
175 g / 6 oz thick-sliced pancetta
or smoked bacon, cubed
50 g / 2 oz / 2 tbsp plain flour
150 ml / ¼ pint / ⅔ cup full-
bodied red wine
300 ml / ½ pint / 1¼ cups beef stock
30 ml / 2 tbsp Marsala
10 ml / 2 tsp dried mixed herbs
salt and freshly ground
black pepper

Serves 8

1

Preheat the oven to 190°C / 375°F / Gas Mark 5. Season the meat well. Heat the olive oil in a large frying pan. When very hot, brown the meat on all sides. Place in a large roasting tin and cook for 1¼ hours.

2

Put the red peppers in the oven to roast for 20 minutes, if small ones are available, or 45 minutes if large ones are used.

3

Near the end of the meat's cooking time, prepare the gravy. Roughly chop the mushroom caps and stems.

4

Heat the frying pan again and add the pancetta or bacon. Cook until the fat runs freely from the meat. Add the flour and cook for a few minutes until browned.

5

Gradually stir in the red wine and the stock. Bring to the boil, stirring. Lower the heat and add the Marsala, herbs and seasoning.

6

Add the mushrooms to the pan and heat through. Remove the sirloin from the oven and leave to stand for 10 minutes before carving it. Serve with the roasted peppers and the hot gravy.

Bacon and Lentil Soup

Serve this hearty soup with chunks of warm, crusty bread.

450 g / 1 lb thick-sliced
bacon, cubed
1 onion, roughly chopped
1 small turnip, roughly chopped
1 celery stick, chopped
1 carrot, sliced
1 potato, peeled and
roughly chopped
75 g / 3 oz / ½ cup lentils
1 bouquet garni
freshly ground black pepper

Serves 4

1

Heat a large pan and add the bacon. Cook for
a few minutes, allowing the fat to run out.

2

Add all the vegetables and cook for
4 minutes.

3

Add the lentils, bouquet garni, seasoning
and enough water to cover. Bring to the boil
and simmer for 1 hour, or until the lentils
are tender.

Creamy Layered Potatoes

Cook the potatoes on the hob first to help the dish to bake more quickly.

INGREDIENTS

*1.5 kg / 3–3 ½ lb large potatoes,
peeled and sliced
2 large onions, sliced
75 g / 3 oz / 6 tbsp unsalted butter
300 ml / ½ pint / 1 ¼ cups double
cream
salt and freshly ground
black pepper*

Serves 6

1

Preheat the oven to 200°C / 400°F /
Gas Mark 6. Blanch the sliced potatoes for 2
minutes, and drain well. Place the potatoes,
onions, butter and cream in a large pan,
stir well and cook for about 15 minutes.

2

Transfer to an ovenproof dish, season and
bake for 1 hour, until the potatoes are tender.

Traditional Beef Stew and Dumplings

This dish can cook in the oven while you go for a wintery walk to work up an appetite.

INGREDIENTS

25 g / 1 oz / 1 tbsp plain flour
1.2 kg / 2½ lb stewing steak,
cubed
30 ml / 2 tbsp olive oil
2 large onions, sliced
450 g / 1 lb carrots, sliced
300 ml / ½ pint / 1¼ cups
Guinness or dark beer
3 bay leaves
10 ml / 2 tsp brown sugar
3 fresh thyme sprigs
5 ml / 1 tsp cider vinegar
salt and freshly ground
black pepper

For the dumplings
115 g / 4 oz / ½ cup grated hard
white fat
225 g / 8 oz / 2 cups self-raising
flour
30 ml / 2 tbsp chopped mixed
fresh herbs
about 150 ml / ¼ pint / ⅔ cup
water

Serves 6

1

Preheat the oven to 160°C / 325°F /
Gas Mark 3. Season the flour and sprinkle
over the meat, tossing to coat.

2

Heat the oil in a large casserole and lightly
sauté the onions and carrots. Remove the
vegetables with a slotted spoon and
reserve them.

3

Brown the meat well in batches
in the casserole.

4

Return all the vegetables to the casserole and
add any leftover seasoned flour. Add the
Guinness or beer, bay leaves, sugar and
thyme. Bring the liquid to the boil and then
transfer to the oven. Leave the meat to cook
for 1 hour and 40 minutes, before making
the dumplings.

5

Mix the grated fat, flour and herbs together.
Add enough water to make a soft
sticky dough.

6

Form the dough into small balls with floured
hands. Add the cider vinegar to the meat and
spoon the dumplings on top. Cook for a
further 20 minutes, until the dumplings
have cooked through, and serve hot.

Country Pie

A classic raised pie. It takes quite a long time to make,
but is a perfect winter treat.

INGREDIENTS

1 small duck
1 small chicken
350 g / 12 oz pork belly, minced
1 egg, lightly beaten
2 shallots, finely chopped
½ tsp ground cinnamon
½ tsp grated nutmeg
5 ml / 1 tsp Worcestershire sauce
finely grated rind of 1 lemon
½ tsp freshly ground black pepper
150 ml / ¼ pint / ⅔ cup red wine
175 g / 6 oz ham, cut into cubes
salt and freshly ground
black pepper

For the jelly
all the meat bones and trimmings
2 carrots
1 onion
2 celery sticks
15 ml / 1 tbsp red wine
1 bay leaf
1 whole clove
1 sachet of gelatine
(about 15 g / 1 oz)

For the pastry
225 g / 8 oz / 1 cup hard white fat
300 ml / ½ pint / 1¼ cups boiling
water
675 g / 1½ lb / 6 cups plain flour
1 egg, lightly beaten with a
pinch of salt

Serves 12

1

Cut as much meat from the raw duck and
chicken as possible, removing the skin and
sinews. Cut the duck and chicken breasts
into cubes and set them aside.

2

Mix the rest of the duck and chicken meat
with the minced pork, egg, shallots, spices,
Worcestershire sauce, lemon rind and salt
and pepper. Add the red wine and leave for
about 15 minutes for the flavours to develop.

3

To make the jelly, place the meat bones and
trimmings, carrots, onion, celery, wine, bay
leaf and clove in a large pan and cover with
2.75 litres / 5 pints / 12½ cups of water.
Bring to the boil, skimming off any scum,
and simmer gently for 2½ hours.

4

To make the pastry, place the fat and water
in a pan and bring to the boil. Sieve the flour
and a pinch of salt into a bowl and pour on the
liquid. Mix with a wooden spoon, and,
when the dough is cool enough to handle,
knead it well and let it sit in a warm place,
covered with a cloth, for 20–30 minutes or
until you are ready to use it. Preheat the
oven to 200°C / 400°F / Gas Mark 6.

5

Grease a 25 cm / 10 in loose-based deep cake tin. Roll out about two-thirds of the pastry thinly enough to line the cake tin. Make sure there are no holes and allow enough pastry to leave a little hanging over the top. Fill the pie with a layer of half the minced-pork mixture; then top this with a layer of the cubed duck and chicken breast-meat and cubes of ham. Top with the remaining minced pork. Brush the overhanging edges of pastry with water and cover with the remaining rolled-out pastry. Seal the edges well. Make two large holes in the top and decorate with any pastry trimmings.

6

Bake the pie for 30 minutes. Brush the top with the egg and salt mixture. Turn down the oven to 180°C / 350°F / Gas Mark 4. After 30 minutes loosely cover the pie with foil to prevent the top getting too brown, and bake it for a further 1 hour.

7

Strain the stock after 2½ hours. Let it cool and remove the solidified layer of fat from the surface. Measure 600 ml / 1 pint / 2½ cups of stock. Heat it gently to just below boiling point and whisk the gelatine into it until no lumps are left. Add the remaining strained stock and leave to cool.

8

When the pie is cool, place a funnel through one of the holes and pour in as much of the stock as possible, letting it come up to the holes in the crust. Leave to set for at least 24 hours before slicing and serving.

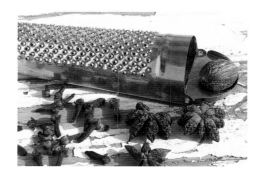

Leek and Onion Tart

This unusual recipe isn't a normal tart with pastry, but an all-in-one savoury slice that is excellent served as an accompaniment to roast meat.

INGREDIENTS

50 g / 2 oz / 4 tbsp unsalted butter
350 g / 12 oz leeks, sliced thinly
225 g / 8 oz / 2 cups self-raising flour
115 g / 4 oz / ½ cup grated hard white fat
150 ml / ¼ pint / ⅔ cup water
salt and freshly ground black pepper

Serves 4

1

Preheat the oven to 200°C / 400°F / Gas Mark 6. Melt the butter in a pan and sauté the leeks until soft. Season well.

2

Mix the flour, fat and water together in a bowl to make a soft but sticky dough. Mix into the leek mixture in the pan. Place in a greased shallow ovenproof dish and bake for 30 minutes, or until brown and crispy. Serve sliced, as a vegetable accompaniment.

Orange Shortbread Fingers

*These are a real tea-time treat. The fingers will keep in an airtight tin
for up to two weeks.*

INGREDIENTS

*115 g / 4 oz / ½ cup unsalted
butter, softened
50 g / 2 oz / 4 tbsp caster sugar,
plus a little extra
finely grated rind of 2 oranges
175 g / 6 oz / 1½ cups plain flour*

Makes 18

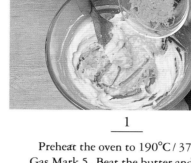

1

Preheat the oven to 190°C / 375°F /
Gas Mark 5. Beat the butter and sugar
together until they are soft and creamy.
Beat in the orange rind.

2

Gradually add the flour and gently pull the
dough together to form a soft ball. Roll the
dough out on a lightly floured surface until
about 1 cm / ½ in thick. Cut it into fingers,
sprinkle over a little extra caster sugar,
prick with a fork and bake for about
20 minutes, or until the fingers are a
light golden colour.

Cranberry Muffins

A tea or breakfast dish that is not too sweet.

INGREDIENTS

350 g / 12 oz / 3 cups plain flour
15 ml / 1 tsp baking powder
pinch of salt
115 g / 4 oz / ½ cup caster sugar
2 eggs
150 ml / ¼ pint / ⅔ cup milk
50 ml / 2 fl oz / 4 tbsp corn oil
finely grated rind of 1 orange
150 g / 5 oz cranberries

Makes 12

1

Preheat the oven to 190°C / 375°F /
Gas Mark 5. Line 12 deep muffin tins with
paper cases. Mix the flour, baking powder,
salt and caster sugar together.

2

Lightly beat the eggs with the milk and oil.
Add them to the dry ingredients and blend
to make a smooth batter. Stir in the orange
rind and cranberries. Divide the mixture
between the muffin cases and bake for
25 minutes until risen and golden.
Leave to cool in the tins for a few minutes,
and serve warm or cold.

Scotch Pancakes

Serve these while still warm, with butter and jam.

INGREDIENTS

*225 g / 8 oz / 2 cups self-raising
flour*
50 g / 2 oz / 4 tbsp caster sugar
50 g / 2 oz / 4 tbsp butter, melted
1 egg
300 ml / ½ pint / 1¼ cups milk
15 g / ½ oz / 1 tbsp hard white fat

Makes 24

1

Mix the flour and sugar together. Add the
melted butter and egg with two-thirds of the
milk. Mix to a smooth batter – it should be
thin enough to find its own level.

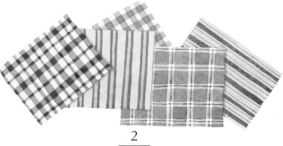

2

Heat a griddle or a heavy-based frying pan
and wipe it with a little hard white fat.
When hot, drop spoonfuls of the mixture
on to the hot griddle or pan. When bubbles
come to the surface of the pancakes, flip them
over to cook until golden on the other side.
Keep the pancakes warm wrapped in a tea
towel while cooking the rest of the mixture.

Christmas Pudding

The classic Christmas dessert. Wrap it in muslin and store it in an airtight container for up to a year for the flavours to develop.

INGREDIENTS

115 g / 4 oz / 1 cup plain flour
pinch of salt
5 ml / 1 tsp ground mixed spice
1/2 tsp ground cinnamon
1/4 tsp freshly grated nutmeg
225 g / 8 oz / 1 cup grated hard white fat
1 dessert apple, grated
225 g / 8 oz / 2 cups fresh white breadcrumbs
350 g / 12 oz / 1⁷/₈ cups soft brown sugar
50 g / 2 oz flaked almonds
225 g / 8 oz / 1 1/2 cups seedless raisins
225 g / 8 oz / 1 1/2 cups currants
225 g / 8 oz / 1 1/2 cups sultanas
115 g / 4 oz ready-to-eat dried apricots
115 g / 4 oz / 3/4 cup chopped mixed peel
finely grated rind and juice of 1 lemon
30 ml / 2 tbsp black treacle
3 eggs
300 ml / 1/2 pint / 1 1/4 cups milk
30 ml / 2 tbsp rum

Serves 8

1

Sieve the flour, salt and spices into a large bowl.

2

Add the fat, apple and other dry ingredients, including the grated lemon rind.

3

Heat the treacle until warm and runny and pour into the dry ingredients.

4

Mix together the eggs, milk, rum and lemon juice.

5

Stir the liquid into the dry mixture.

6

Spoon the mixture into two 1.2 litre / 2 pint / 5 cup basins. Overwrap the puddings with pieces of greaseproof paper, pleated to allow for expansion, and tie with string. Steam the puddings in a steamer or saucepan of boiling water. Each pudding needs 10 hours' cooking and 3 hours' reheating. Remember to keep the water level topped up to keep the pans from boiling dry. Serve decorated with holly.

Gifts from the Pantry

Make the most of seasonal fruits and vegetables, by making jams, jellies and preserves to enjoy the year round, or to give as gifts. Country favourites include strawberry jam, apple or mint jelly, or piccalilli.

Apple and Mint Jelly

This jelly is delicious served with garden peas, as well as the more traditional rich roasted meat such as lamb.

INGREDIENTS

900 g / 2 lb Bramley cooking apples
granulated sugar
45 ml / 3 tbsp chopped fresh mint

Makes 3 × 450 g / 1 lb jars

1

Chop the apples roughly and put them in a preserving pan.

2

Add enough water to cover. Simmer until the fruit is soft.

3

Pour through a jelly bag, allowing it to drip overnight. Do not squeeze the bag or the jelly will become cloudy.

4

Measure the amount of juice. To every 600 ml / 1 pint / 2½ cups of juice, add 500 g / 1¼ lb / 2¾ cups granulated sugar.

5

Place the juice and sugar in a large pan and heat gently. Dissolve the sugar and then bring to the boil. Test for setting, by pouring about 15 ml / 1 tbsp into a saucer and leaving to cool slightly. If a wrinkle forms on the surface when pushed with a fingertip, the jelly will set. When a set is reached, leave to cool.

6

Stir in the mint and pot into sterilized jars. Seal each jar with a waxed disc and a tightly fitting cellophane top. Store in a cool, dark place. The jelly will keep unopened for up to a year. Once opened, keep in the fridge and consume within a week.

Lemon and Lime Curd

Serve this creamy, tangy spread with toast or muffins,
instead of jam, for a delightful change.

INGREDIENTS

115 g / 4 oz / ½ cup   grated rind and juice of 2 lemons
unsalted butter   grated rind and juice of 2 limes
3 eggs   225 g / 8 oz / 1⅛ cups caster sugar

Makes 2 × 450 g / 1 lb jars

1

Set a heatproof mixing bowl over a large pan
of simmering water. Add the butter.

2

Lightly beat the eggs and add them
to the butter.

3

Add the lemon and lime rinds and juices,
then add the sugar.

4

Stir the mixture constantly until it thickens.
Pour into sterilized jars. Seal each jar with a
waxed disc and a tightly fitting cellophane top.
Store in a cool, dark place. The curd will
keep unopened for up to a month.
Once opened, keep in the fridge and
consume within a week.

Poached Spiced Plums in Brandy

Bottling spiced fruit is a great way to preserve summer flavours for eating in winter. Serve these with whipped cream as a dessert.

INGREDIENTS

600 ml / 1 pint / 2½ cups brandy
rind of 1 lemon, peeled in a long strip
350 g / 12 oz / 1⅔ cups caster sugar
1 cinnamon stick
900 g / 2 lb fresh plums

Makes 900 g / 2 lb

1

Put the brandy, lemon rind, sugar and cinnamon stick in a large pan and heat gently to dissolve the sugar. Add the plums and poach for 15 minutes, or until soft. Remove with a slotted spoon.

2

Reduce the syrup by a third by rapid boiling. Strain it over the plums. Bottle the plums in large sterilized jars. Seal tightly and store for up to 6 months in a cool, dark place.

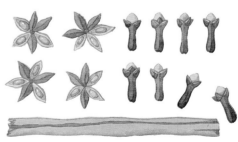

Spiced Pickled Pears

These delicious pears are the perfect accompaniment for cooked ham
or cold meat salads.

900 g / 2 lb pears
600 ml / 1 pint / 2½ cups
white-wine vinegar
225 g / 8 oz / 1⅛ cups caster sugar
1 cinnamon stick
5 star anise
10 whole cloves

Makes 900 g / 2 lb

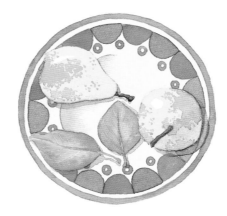

1

Peel the pears, keeping them whole
and leaving on the stalks. Heat the vinegar
and sugar together until the sugar has melted.
Pour over the pears and poach for 15 minutes.

2

Add the cinnamon, star anise and cloves
and simmer for 10 minutes. Remove the
pears and pack tightly into sterilized jars.
Simmer the syrup for a further 15 minutes
and pour it over the pears. Seal the jars
tightly and store in a cool, dark place. The
pears will keep for up to a year unopened.
Once opened, store in the fridge and
consume within a week.

Tomato Chutney

*This spicy chutney is delicious with a selection of cheeses and biscuits,
or with cold meats.*

INGREDIENTS

900 g / 2 lb tomatoes, skinned
225 g / 8 oz / 1⅓ cups raisins
225 g / 8 oz onions, chopped

225 g / 8 oz / 1⅛ cups caster sugar
600 ml / 1 pint / 2½ cups
malt vinegar

Makes 4 × 450 g / 1 lb jars

1

Chop the tomatoes roughly. Put them in
a preserving pan.

2

Add the raisins, onions and caster sugar.

3

Pour over the vinegar. Bring to the boil
and let it simmer for 2 hours, uncovered.
Pot into sterilized jars. Seal with a waxed disc
and cover with a tightly fitting cellophane
top. Store in a cool, dark place. The chutney
will keep unopened for up to a year. Once
opened, store in the fridge and consume
within a week.

Strawberry Jam

This classic recipe is always popular. Make sure the jam is allowed to cool before pouring into jars so the fruit doesn't float to the top.

1.5 kg / 3–3½ lb strawberries
juice of ½ lemon
1.5 kg / 3–3½ lb granulated sugar

Makes about 2.25 kg / 5 lb

1

Hull the strawberries.

2

Put the strawberries in a pan with the lemon juice. Mash a few of the strawberries. Let the fruit simmer for 20 minutes or until softened.

3

Add the sugar and let it dissolve slowly over a gentle heat. Then let the jam boil rapidly until a setting point is reached.

4

Leave to stand until the strawberries are well distributed through the jam. Pot into sterilized jars. Seal each jar with a waxed disc and cover with a tightly fitting cellophane top. Store in a cool dark place. The jam may be kept unopened for up to a year. Once opened, keep in the fridge and consume within a week.

Three-fruit Marmalade

Home-made marmalade may be time-consuming but the results are incomparably better than store-bought varieties.

INGREDIENTS

350 g / 12 oz oranges
350 g / 12 oz lemons
700 g / 1½ lb grapefruit
2.5 litres / 4½ pints / 10¼ cups water
2.75 kg / 6 lb granulated sugar

Makes 6 × 450 g / 1 lb jars

1

Rinse and dry the fruit.

2

Put the fruit in a preserving pan. Add the water and let it simmer for about 2 hours.

3

Quarter the fruit, remove the pulp and add it to the pan with the cooking liquid.

4

Cut the rinds into slivers, and add to the pan. Add the sugar. Gently heat until the sugar has dissolved. Bring to the boil and cook until a setting point is reached. Leave to stand for 1 hour to allow the peel to settle. Pour into sterilized jars. Seal each jar with a waxed disc and a tightly fitting cellophane top. Store in a cool, dark place.

Piccalilli

The piquancy of this relish partners well with sausages, bacon or ham.

INGREDIENTS

675 g / 1½ lb cauliflower   5 ml / 1 tsp dry mustard powder
450 g / 1 lb small onions   10 ml / 2 tsp cornflour
350 g / 12 oz French beans   600 ml / 1 pint / 2½ cups vinegar
5 ml / 1 tsp ground turmeric

Makes 3 × 450 g / 1 lb jars

1

Cut the cauliflower into tiny florets.

2

Peel the onions and top and tail
the French beans.

3

In a small saucepan, measure in the turmeric,
mustard powder and cornflour, and pour
over the vinegar. Stir well and simmer
for 10 minutes.

4

Pour the vinegar mixture over the vegetables
in a pan, mix well and simmer
for 45 minutes.

5

Pour into sterilized jars. Seal each jar with a
waxed disc and a tightly fitting cellophane
top. Store in a cool dark place. The piccalilli
will keep unopened for up to a year. Once
opened store in the fridge and consume
within a week.

Rosemary-flavoured Oil

This pungent oil is ideal drizzled over meat or vegetables before grilling.

600 ml / 1 pint / 2½ cups olive oil
5 fresh rosemary sprigs

Makes 600 ml / 1 pint / 2½ cups

1

Heat the oil until warm but not too hot.

2

Add four rosemary sprigs and heat gently.
Put the reserved rosemary sprig in a clean
bottle. Strain the oil, pour in the bottle and
seal tightly. Allow to cool and store in a
cool, dark place. Use within a week.

Thyme-flavoured Vinegar

This vinegar is delicious sprinkled over salmon intended for poaching.

600 ml / 1 pint / 2½ cups
white-wine vinegar
5 fresh thyme sprigs
3 garlic cloves, peeled

Makes 600 ml / 1 pint / 2½ cups

1

Warm the vinegar.

2

Add four thyme sprigs and the garlic and
heat gently. Put the reserved thyme sprig in
a clean bottle, strain the vinegar, and add to
the bottle. Seal tightly, allow to cool and
store in a cool, dark place. The vinegar
may be kept unopened for up to 3 months.

Index